Monday

1. 8 + 2 = _____

4. $0 + \boxed{} = 9$

2. 9
  − 3
  _____

5. There were 17 girls in Mrs. Baker's class last year. This year there are 9 girls. How many more girls were in her class last year?

_____ girls

3. Fill in the correct symbol.

< = >

Tuesday ⟨ 1 ⟩

1. 0 + 10 = _____

4. Write the number for twenty.

_____

2. 13
  − 6
  _____

5. Tina saw a movie about parrots. There were 8 parrots sitting in a tree, and then 6 more landed on the branches. Then 4 flew away. How many parrots were still in the tree?

_____ parrots

3. Color $\frac{1}{8}$.

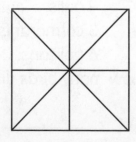

Wednesday ⟨ 1 ⟩

1. 11 − 7 = _____

2. 4
      + 9

3. Mark the eighth dot.

◯◯◯◯◯◯◯◯◯◯

4. Count by ones to fill in the missing numbers.

____ 100 ____

____ 149 ____

____ 63 ____

____ 102 ____

5. If a muffin costs 7¢, how much will 3 muffins cost?

_____¢

Thursday ⟨ 1 ⟩

1. 12 − 6 = _____

2. 5
      + 7

3. Continue the pattern.

11 13 15 ____ ____ ____

4. What time is it?

quarter past _____

5. On a walk along the beach, Jarod saw

9 gulls,
3 cormorants, and
6 pelicans.
How many birds did he see?

_____ birds

Friday ⟨1⟩

Complete each number sentence. Use only 3, 4, and 5.

$$\underline{\hspace{1cm}} + \underline{\hspace{1cm}} + \underline{\hspace{1cm}} = 12$$

$$\underline{\hspace{1cm}} + \underline{\hspace{1cm}} - \underline{\hspace{1cm}} = 6$$

$$\underline{\hspace{1cm}} + \underline{\hspace{1cm}} - \underline{\hspace{1cm}} = 4$$

Daily Progress Record ⟨1⟩

How many did you get correct each day? Color the squares.

	Monday	Tuesday	Wednesday	Thursday	Friday
5					▓
4					▓
3					
2					
1					

1. 4 + 7 = _____

2.   11
     − 6
    ———

3. Count by tens.

50 ____ ____ ____

____ ____

4. What fraction is shaded?

$\dfrac{1}{6}$ $\dfrac{1}{3}$ $\dfrac{1}{4}$ $\dfrac{1}{2}$

5. Tasha practiced her dance for 2 hou
before lunch and 3 hours after lunch
How many hours did she practice?

_____ hours

---

1. 10 − 2 = _____

2.   9
     + 3
    ———

3. What time is it?

____ : ____

4. 6 + ☐ = 15

5. Write a word problem for this picture

_____

_____

_____

1. 18 − 9 = _____

2.   6
   + 8
   ____

3. Mark the shapes with no corners.

4. Write the number for one hundred.

   _____

5. On Monday Bob saw 7 deer in the meadow. On Friday he saw 8 deer. Yesterday he saw 4 more deer. How many deer did Bob see?

   _____ deer

---

1. 9 + 8 = _____

2.   16
   − 4
   ____

3. Write the numbers in order.

   6   42   17   88   3

   ____ ____ ____ ____ ____

4. 9 + 5 = 14, so ☐ − 5 = 9.

5. Asian elephants can be as tall as 9 feet. African elephants can be as tall as 12 feet. How much taller can the African elephant be?

   _____ feet

Friday ⟨2⟩

Mrs. Garcia has taught third grade for 9 years. Mr. Lee taught third grade for 7 years and then fourth grade for 6 years. How much longer has Mr. Lee taught than Mrs. Garcia?

Show your work here.

Write your answer here.

Daily Math Practice

Daily Progress Record ⟨2⟩

How many did you get correct each day? Color the squares.

	Monday	Tuesday	Wednesday	Thursday	Friday
5					
4					
3					
2					
1					

EMC 6713 • © Evan-Moor Corp

Monday ⟨3⟩

1. $25 + 5 =$ _____

2. $\begin{array}{r} 18 \\ -\ 3 \\ \hline \end{array}$

3. Mark the even numbers.

     1   2   3   4   5   6   7   8   9

4. thirteen – five = _____

5. Rainbow stickers cost 10¢ each. How much did it cost Jill to buy 9 stickers?

         _____¢

Tuesday ⟨3⟩

1. $56 - 5 =$ _____

2. $\begin{array}{r} 7 \\ +\ 9 \\ \hline \end{array}$

3. Name these shapes.

    a. _____

    b. _____

    c. _____

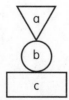

4. $9 +$ ☐ $= 13$

5. The mother giraffe is 8 meters tall. Her baby is 3 meters tall. How much taller is the mother?

     _____ meters

Wednesday ⟨**3**⟩

1. 32 + 8 = _____

2. 18
  – 6

3.

  = _____ ¢

4. Fill in the correct symbol.

  < = >

  169 ◯ 183

5. Scout Troop 27 went on a trip to a farm. They left at 9:00. The trip took 2 hours. Show the time they arrived at the farm.

Thursday ⟨**3**⟩

1. 14 + 3 = _____

2. 20
  – 7

3. Are both sides the same?

  yes
  no

 yes
  no

4. Count by twos.

  90 ____ ____ ____

  ____ ____

5. There are 18 students on Ryan's team. Half are boys. How many boys are there on his team?

  _____ boys

  EMC 6713 • © Evan-Moor Corp.

Friday ⬡3

Make 12 in each direction.
Use these numbers: 1 2̶ 3 4̶ 5̶ 6 7

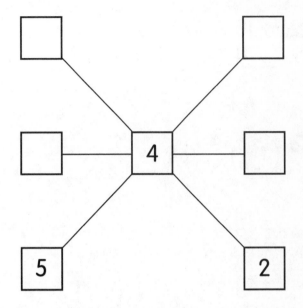

Daily Progress Record ⬡3

How many did you get correct each day? Color the squares.

	Monday	Tuesday	Wednesday	Thursday	Friday
5					
4					
3					
2					
1					

Monday ⟨4⟩

1. 14 − 7 = _____

2.   10
       + 4
       ‾‾‾‾

3. + = _____ ¢

4. 12 + 6 = 6 + ☐

5. Watermelon costs 5¢ a pound. How much does a 9-pound watermelon cost?

_____ ¢

Tuesday ⟨4⟩

1. 4 + 8 + 2 = _____

2.   20
       − 0
       ‾‾‾‾

3. Continue the pattern.

 ___ ___ ___ ___

4. twelve + seven = _____

5. Morris bought 6 toy cars, a kite, and 9 marbles. How many toys did he buy?

_____ toys

1. 12 − 2 = _____

2.   6
    + 5
    ———

3. What is the best estimate for the
   answer to 98 + 49 = ?

   a. 160   b. 140   c. 150

4. Continue the pattern.

   100 200 ____ ____ ____

5. Tammy has two cats. Fluffy weighs
   3 pounds less than Pete. If Pete
   weighs 9 pounds, how much does
   Fluffy weigh?

   _____ pounds

---

1. 18 − 8 = _____

2.   7
    + 9
    ———

3. How long is this crayon?

   _____ inches

4. Fill in the correct symbol.

   < = >

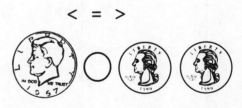

5. Jamal rides his bike to school and
   back home. It is two miles each way.
   How many miles does he ride in five
   days?

   _____ miles

Friday ⟨4⟩

Look at the graph to help you answer the questions.

Favorite Cookies		
Oreo® 🍪	🍪 🍪 🍪 🍪	
chocolate chip 🍪	🍪 🍪 🍪 🍪 🍪 🍪 🍪	
oatmeal 🍪	🍪 🍪	
peanut butter 🍪	🍪 🍪 🍪 ◗	
Fig Newton® 🍪		

🍪 = 2   ◗ = 1

1. How many different kinds of cookies are on the graph? _____

2. How many kids chose chocolate chip? _____

3. Which cookie did no one pick? _____

Daily Math Practice

Daily Progress Record ⟨4⟩

How many did you get correct each day? Color the squares.

	Monday	Tuesday	Wednesday	Thursday	Friday
5					
4					
3					
2					
1					

EMC 6713 · © Evan-Moor Corp.

Monday 5

1. $8 \times 2 =$ _____

2.
$$\begin{array}{r} 29 \\ -5 \\ \hline \end{array}$$

3. Color $\frac{4}{8}$.

4. 7 tens and 4 ones = _____

5. Bert bought 2 cookies that cost 10¢ each. He gave the clerk a quarter. How much money did he get back?

a. 5¢   b. 10¢   c. 15¢   d. 20¢

Tuesday 5

1. $5 + 8 + 6 =$ _____

2. $9 \div 3 =$ _____

3. Circle the names for 12.

4 + 8   6 + 6   13 − 4

5 + 9   4 x 3   twelve

4. Write the missing numbers.

116 ____ ____ 119 ____ ____

5. Amy and her parents went on a sailing vacation. It was sunny 9 days of the trip, foggy 2 days, and stormy 3 days. How long were they on vacation?

_____ days

1. 38 + 21 = _____

2. 27
    − 12
   ‾‾‾‾

3. Write the time on the clock.

a quarter past 3

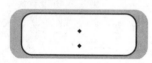

4. Mark the odd numbers.

1   2   3   4   5   6   7   8

5. The explorers needed to hike 19 miles in one day. They hiked 8 miles in the morning. They hiked 6 miles in the afternoon. How far did they still need to go?

_____ miles

---

1. 80 − 4 = _____

2. $5\overline{)5}$

3. How long is it?

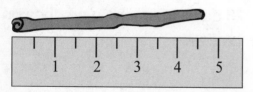

_____ cm

4. Fill in the correct symbol.

< = >

699 ◯ 966

5. A baby elephant is about 3 feet tall when it is born. How much will the elephant have to grow to be 12 feet tall as an adult?

_____ feet

EMC 6713 • © Evan-Moor Corp.

Friday 5

1. Make an **X** on the fifth clown.

2. Circle the eighth clown.

3. Draw a red hat on the second clown.

4. Draw a line under the fourth clown.

5. In what position is the last clown?

   twentieth   ninth   twelfth

Daily Math Practice

Daily Progress Record 5

How many did you get correct each day? Color the squares.

	Monday	Tuesday	Wednesday	Thursday	Friday
5					
4					
3					
2					
1					

Monday 6

1. $14 \div 2 =$ _____

2.
$$\begin{array}{r} 21 \\ 30 \\ + 17 \\ \hline \end{array}$$

3. What is the perimeter of this chicken coop?

_____

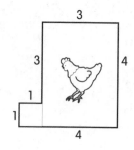

4. Which of these is heaviest?

○ car ○ bus ○ motorcycle

5. Maurice bought a collar, a catnip mouse, and a bag of kitty litter for his new pet. He gave the clerk $15. If he got back $3 in change, how much did he spend?

$_____

Tuesday 6

1. $14 + 9 =$ _____

2.
$$\begin{array}{r} 8 \\ \times 4 \\ \hline \end{array}$$

3. Circle the amount.

a. 73¢   b. 68¢   c. 83¢

4. $17 \ \boxed{} \ 9 = 8$

5. The ball game started at 10:00. It lasted one and a half hours. Show what time the game ended.

Started   Ended

EMC 6713 • © Evan-Moor Corp.

1. 16 + 12 = _____

2.   30
   − 4
   ‾‾‾‾

3. Which of these numbers is one hundred sixteen?

   ○ 161   ○ 160   ○ 116

4. Write these in the correct order.

   fourth   _____

   second   _____

   first   _____

   third   _____

5. Nine boys, eight girls, and two teachers played ball at recess. How many people played ball?

   _____ people

1. 41 − 9 = _____

2.   18
  + 7
  ‾‾‾‾

3. = _____

4. Fill in the correct symbol.

   < = >

   2 cups ◯ 1 quart

5. One windy day, 25 hot-air balloons went up into the air. Then 7 of them landed. How many were still in the air?

   _____ hot-air balloons

Friday 〈 6 〉

Mom made two large pizzas for Albert and his friends to have Saturday night. Three boys came over. Show how Mom cut the pizzas so each boy could have three pieces.

Daily Math Practice

Daily Progress Record 〈 6 〉

How many did you get correct each day? Color the squares.

	Monday	Tuesday	Wednesday	Thursday	Friday
5					
4					
3					
2					
1					

1. 38 − 9 = _____

2. 27
     + 10

3. Mark the scale that is used to weigh a person.

4. Count by fives.

75 ____ ____ ____ ____ ____

5. If Jo Ellen has 14 socks, how many pairs does she have?

_____ pairs

---

1. 6 ÷ 3 = _____

2. 3
     × 5

3. Congruent figures are exactly the same. Are these shapes congruent?

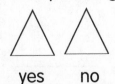

yes   no

4. Count by ones to fill in the missing numbers.

____ 420 ____

____ 399 ____

5. Write a word problem for the number sentence 2 × 2 = 4.

_____

_____

_____

1. 12 − 10 = _____

2.   12
      + 0
     _____

3. Write four names for 14.

_____   _____

_____   _____

4. A triangle _____ has three sides.

   a. sometimes

   b. never

   c. always

5. An octopus has eight tentacles. If the octopus wore gloves, how many pairs would it need?

_____ pairs

---

1. 16 + 9 = _____

2.   40
      − 28
     _____

3. 1 hundred + 6 tens + 9 ones =

_____

4. Choose the best answer. Which unit of measurement would you use to tell how much an apple weighs?

   a. ounces   c. pounds

   b. tons   d. quarts

5. There were 4 clowns, 3 astronauts, 2 cowboys, and 5 monsters. How many children came to the costume party?

_____ children

Fill in the boxes.

Cats	1	2	3	4	5
ears	2				
legs	4				
whiskers	6				

Daily Progress Record ⟨7⟩

How many did you get correct each day? Color the squares.

	Monday	Tuesday	Wednesday	Thursday	Friday
5					
4					
3					
2					
1					

1. 12 ÷ 3 = _____

2.   25
     − 10

3. Write four names for 15.

_____   _____

_____   _____

4. How many sides are in a rectangle?

_____

How many corners are in a rectangle

_____

5. Mother sent Jessie and Cal to pick corn for supper. Jessie picked 6 ears. Cal picked twice as many ears as Jessie. How many ears of corn did they have for supper?

_____ ears of corn

1. 16 + 34 = _____

2.   12
     − 10

3. Draw an AABCC pattern.

4. What is this number?

two hundred sixteen

a. 20,016   b. 216   c. 206

5. Ellen had twelve pennies. She gave one-fourth of the pennies to Will. How many did she keep?

_____ pennies

EMC 6713 • © Evan-Moor Corp

Wednesday 8

1. 20 + 36 = _____

2. 17
    − 9
    _____

3. Mark the units of measure used to measure water.

gallon   meter   pound

cup   liter   ounce

4. Fill in the correct symbol.

< = >

314 ◯ 304

5. Jack rode the bus to see his grandmother on Saturday. It was 16 blocks from his house there and 16 blocks back home. How many blocks did he travel?

_____ blocks

Thursday 8

1. 45 − 25 = _____

2. 3
    × 4
    _____

3. Are the sides symmetrical?

yes   no

4. 12 + 2 = 14, so 14 − ☐ = 12.

5. Grandma was making a cake for the family picnic. It had to bake for 45 minutes. She put it in the oven at 2:00. Show the time she took the cake out of the oven.

☐ : ☐

Friday ⟨8⟩

Margaret asked 10 people, "What kind of pet do you have?" Record their answers on this graph.

dog 𝍬 /
cat 𝍬
fish ///
hamster 𝍬
snake /

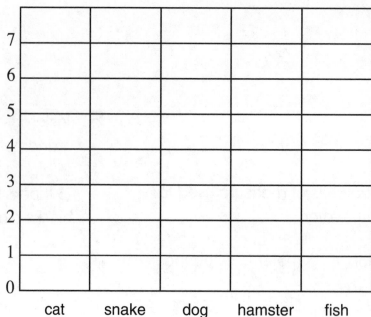

Daily Progress Record ⟨8⟩

How many did you get correct each day? Color the squares.

	Monday	Tuesday	Wednesday	Thursday	Friday
5					
4					
3					
2					
1					

EMC 6713 • © Evan-Moor Corp

Monday 9

1. 6 × 4 = _____

4. 23 + 7 = 30, so ☐ − 7 = 23.

2.   48
      − 19

5. Write number sentences using 7, 5, and 12.

____ − ____ = ____

____ − ____ = ____

____ + ____ = ____

____ + ____ = ____

3. Mara's baby brother weighs 11 pounds. Mara weighs 77 pounds. What is the difference in their weights?

_____ pounds

Tuesday 9

1. 15 ÷ 5 = _____

4. Continue the pattern.

19 23 27 ____ ____ ____ 43

2.   234
      + 53

5. Max and Stan went to the store. It took them 20 minutes to get there, 15 minutes to shop, and 20 minutes to get home. How long were they gone?

_____ minutes

3. Color $\frac{2}{3}$.

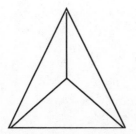

1. $18 = 3 + 5 +$ _____

2. $\begin{array}{r} 80 \\ -\ 39 \\ \hline \end{array}$

3. Which number is six hundred three?

63   630   603   6,300

4. Count by threes.

9 12 _____ _____ _____

_____ _____

5. Jay had 65¢. He spent a quarter. How much money did he have left?

_____¢

---

1. $37 + 54 =$ _____

2. $\begin{array}{r} 3 \\ \times\ 6 \\ \hline \end{array}$

3. Name the shape.

a. rectangle   b. pentagon   c. hexagon

4. $2 \times 6 = 6 \times \boxed{}$

5. How many doughnuts are in $\frac{1}{2}$ dozen?

_____ doughnuts

   EMC 6713 • © Evan-Moor Corp

Friday ⟨9⟩

November						
Sun	Mon	Tues	Wed	Thurs	Fri	Sat
	1	2	3	4	5	6
7	8	9	10	11	12	13
14	15	16	17	18	19	20
21	22	23	24	25	26	27
28	29	30				

1. What day of the week is November 25? _____

2. What day comes after Saturday? _____

3. What is the date of the third Thursday? _____

Daily Progress Record ⟨9⟩

How many did you get correct each day? Color the squares.

	Monday	Tuesday	Wednesday	Thursday	Friday
5					
4					
3					
2					
1					

1. $4 \times 4 =$ _____

2. 37
       − 8

3. Mark 45¢.

4. Circle each digit in the tens place.

29   57   89

5. Four students brought their teacher flowers. If each student gave the teacher three flowers, how many did she get?

_____ flowers

1. $52 - 18 =$ _____

2. 456
      + 153

3. Write the number for thirty-six.

_____

4. Read the time. Show 15 minutes later.

5. The cook needs a dozen eggs to make an angel food cake. If he has 8 eggs, how many more does he need?

_____ eggs

EMC 6713 • © Evan-Moor Corp

Wednesday 〈10〉

1. 60 – 40 = _____

2. 193
      + 26

3. Which is the best estimate for the answer to this problem?

106 – 49

a. 50   b. 70   c. 100

4. Fill in the correct symbol.

< = >

963 ◯ 639

5. A cheetah can run 60 miles per hour for a short distance. A greyhound dog can run 40 miles per hour. How much faster can the cheetah run?

_____ miles per hour

Thursday 〈10〉

1. 18 ÷ 6 = _____

2. 138
      + 91

3. eighteen – fifteen = _____

4. How much is shaded?

◯ $\frac{2}{3}$ ◯ $\frac{1}{2}$ ◯ $\frac{3}{4}$

5. If marbles cost 5¢ each, how much will six marbles cost?

_____ ¢

Friday ⟨10⟩

Maria is repairing her old bike. She bought new tires for $20, a bell for $5, and a basket for $13. How much did she spend?

$_____

If Maria gives the clerk $40, how much money will she get back?

$_____

Daily Math Practice

Daily Progress Record ⟨10⟩

How many did you get correct each day? Color the squares.

	Monday	Tuesday	Wednesday	Thursday	Friday
5					
4					
3					
2					
1					

EMC 6713 · © Evan-Moor Corp

1. $7 + 3 + 9 =$ _____

2. 52
  $-\ 36$

3. Mark the parallelogram.

4. $56 - 32 = 24$, so $56 - 24 =$ ☐ .

5. Carnival ride tickets are 10 for $1. How many can Sue buy for $4?

_____ tickets

---

1. $93 - 36 =$ _____

2. 52
  $+\ 39$

3. Continue the pattern.

400 450 500 ____ ____

____ ____

4. $5\ \boxed{}\ 7 = 35$

5. Roberto found a sale on dog food. Each can cost 40¢. How much did he pay for five cans?

$_____._____

1. 85 + 7 = _____

2. 5$\overline{)35}$

3. Fill in the correct symbol.

< = >

8 dimes ◯ 1 half dollar

4. thirty-five ☐ twelve = twenty-three

5. Eight people went on a beach picnic Each person drank three cups of lemonade. How many cups of lemonade did they drink?

_____ cups

1. 4 × 7 = _____

2. 326
    – 109

3. Mark the names for 10.

5 × 2   50 – 40

8 + 3   20 ÷ 2

4. What ordinal number comes before sixteenth?

_____

5. Marcus had 15 toy cars. He kept the cars in 3 boxes. Each box held the same number of cars. How many cars were in a box?

_____ cars

EMC 6713 • © Evan-Moor Corp

Friday 11

$60 - 20 + 30 + 50 - 40 = $ _____

Show your work here.

Write your answer here.

Daily Math Practice

Daily Progress Record 〈11〉

How many did you get correct each day? Color the squares.

	Monday	Tuesday	Wednesday	Thursday	Friday
5					
4					
3					
2					
1					

Monday ⟨12⟩

1. 32 + 52 + 12 = _____

2.   534
      – 380

3. Circle the digit in the tens place.
   Make an **X** on the digit in the
   ones place.

                83

4. Mark the odd numbers.

      12   11   15   10

5. Sara cut five brownies into fourths.
   How many pieces did she have?

   _____ pieces

Tuesday ⟨12⟩

1. 41 – 29 = _____

2.   756
      + 223

3. 4 x 5 = 20, so 20 ÷ 5 = ☐ .

4. Write these numbers in order.

   nineteenth _____

   fifteenth   _____

   eleventh   _____

5. Today 67 students are going on
   a field trip. A bus holds 50 children.
   How many buses will be needed?

   _____ buses

          EMC 6713 • © Evan-Moor Cor

Wednesday 12

1. $5{,}972 + 0 =$ _____

2.   5
    × 6

3. Color $\frac{3}{8}$.

4. Write the missing numbers.

____ 257 258 ____ ____ ____

5. Bananas are on sale two for 25¢. How much will 6 bananas cost?

_____¢

Thursday 12

1. $96 - 26 =$ _____

2.   65
    + 25

3.
     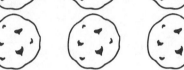

= _____¢

4. 28 ☐ 4 = 7

5. It takes 2 tablespoons of peanut butter and 3 tablespoons of jelly to make a sandwich. How much peanut butter and jelly would be needed for 8 sandwiches?

_____ Tbsp. peanut butter

_____ Tbsp. jelly

Friday ⟨12⟩

1. What food do half of the people like best? _____

2. What is the least favorite? _____

3. Which of these foods do you like best?

    a. hamburger and fries

    b. taco

    c. pizza

    d. none of these

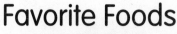

Favorite Foods

Daily Math Practice

Daily Progress Record ⟨12⟩

How many did you get correct each day? Color the squares.

	Monday	Tuesday	Wednesday	Thursday	Friday
5					
4					
3					
2					
1					

EMC 6713 • © Evan-Moor Cor

1. 58 + 35 + 12 = _____

2. 63
     – 27

3. Mark the cube.

4. Continue the pattern.

45 43 41 _____ _____

_____ _____

5. Mary had nine books. One-third of the books were fairy tales. How many books were fairy tales?

_____ books

1. 100 – 40 = _____

2. 654
     – 492

3. _____ corners

_____ faces

_____ edges

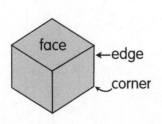

4. Count by ones to write the missing numbers.

_____ 399 _____

_____ 600 _____

5. Jeff went to the circus and saw a minibus full of clowns. He watched as 12 clowns got out of the bus and 27 clowns stayed inside the bus. How many clowns were there in all?

_____ clowns

1. $24 \div 6 =$ _____

2. $\begin{array}{r} 6 \\ \times 7 \\ \hline \end{array}$

3. Tyrone bought two cans of paint. The green paint cost $2.57. The white paint cost $4.35. How much did he spend on the paint?

$ _____

4.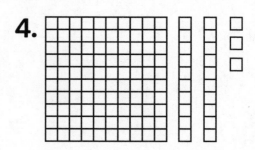

_____ hundred + _____ tens

+ _____ ones = _____

5. Write the number name for 27.

_____

1. $88 - 49 =$ _____

2. $\begin{array}{r} 792 \\ + 133 \\ \hline \end{array}$

3. Continue the pattern.

6 12 18 ____ ____ ____ ____

____ ____

4. $20 + 16 = 36$, so $36 - \boxed{} = 2$

5. Mei Lee dropped her purse and spilled her money. She found 1 quarter, 4 dimes, 3 nickels, and 13 pennies. How much did she find?

_____ ¢

EMC 6713 • © Evan-Moor Corp

Friday 13

tart — 50¢

cupcake — 10¢

brownie — 25¢

cookie — 5¢

1. How much will two cupcakes and a brownie cost? _____¢

2. How much will a tart and four cupcakes cost? _____¢

3. How much will a dozen cookies cost? _____¢

Daily Progress Record 13

How many did you get correct each day? Color the squares.

	Monday	Tuesday	Wednesday	Thursday	Friday
5					
4					
3					
2					
1					

1. 248 + 354 = _____

2.   736
       − 255

3. Mark the trapezoid.

4. Continue the pattern.

122 124 ____ ____ ____

5. Stella made a bouquet of flowers for her mother. She used 13 yellow tulips, 2 white carnations, and 6 red roses. How many flowers did she use in the bouquet?

_____ flowers

1. 21 ÷ 7 = _____

2.   659
       + 324

3. Draw an ABAC pattern.

4. Are these shapes congruent?

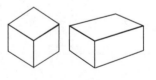

yes   no

5. Tickets cost $3 for children and $7 for adults. How much will tickets cost for a family of 3 children and 2 adults?

$_____

Wednesday ⟨14⟩

1. $90 + 40 - 70 =$ _____

4. $4 \times 9 = 36$, so $36 \div \boxed{} = 4$.

2.   5
     $\times\ 7$

5. Three third-grade classes are going on a field trip. Two classes each have 28 students and one class has 26 students. How many students are going on the trip?

_____ students

3. Draw a line of symmetry.

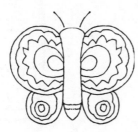

Thursday ⟨14⟩

1. $12,461 - 0 =$ _____

4. Write three names for 24.

_____

_____

_____

2.   436
     $+\ \ 87$

3. twenty-nine – zero =

_____

5. On Saturday, 75 kids went to the beach and 48 kids went swimming. How many kids did <u>not</u> swim?

_____ kids

Sal and Cody needed money to go to a concert. Sal earned $9.38 walking dogs. Cody earned $6.62 collecting cans and bottles. How much money did they have?

$_____

If they need $18.00 for two tickets, how much more money do they need?

$_____

Daily Progress Record ⟨14⟩

How many did you get correct each day? Color the squares.

	Monday	Tuesday	Wednesday	Thursday	Friday
5					
4					
3					
2					
1					

Monday ⬡15

1. 45 ÷ 5 = _____

2.   200
      + 600

3. 3 hours = _____ minutes

_____ hours = 1 day

4. Count by twos.

364 366 ____ ____ ____

____

5. Ed has 26 stuffed animals and Jill has 39. How many stuffed animals do they have? Mark the way you would solve the problem.

a. add   c. multiply

b. subtract   d. divide

Tuesday ⬡15

1. (18 – 9) x 4 = _____

2.   643
      – 471

3. What units of measure could you use to measure juice?

a. centimeters   c. liters

b. ounces   d. pounds

4. Where does the decimal belong in one dollar and 27 cents?

$127

5. There are 3 glasses of water in each liter bottle. How many liters would 9 people need if they drank 2 glasses each?

_____ liters

Wednesday ⟨15⟩

1. 126 – 120 = _____

2.
```
  249
+ 460
```

3. What is the perimeter of this shape?

6 cm

4 cm   5 cm

9 cm

_____

4. 6 x 5 = 30, so 5 x ☐ = 30.

5. Jasmine baked 2 dozen chocolate chip cookies, 1 dozen oatmeal cookies, and 1 dozen peanut butter cookies for her party. How many cookies did she bake?

_____ cookies

Thursday ⟨15⟩

1. 5 x 6 = _____

2. two hundred + three hundred =

_____

3. Mrs. Chang made 137 jars of jam. She sold 93 jars. How many jars does she have left?

_____ jars of jam

4. How many inches are in one foot?

   a. 18   b. 14   c. 12

5. Are these two shapes congruent?

   yes   no

Give a reason for your answer.

_____

_____

   EMC 6713 • © Evan-Moor Corp.

Friday 15

Make 15 in each direction.
Use these numbers: 1 2 3 4̶ 5 6 7̶ 8̶ 9̶

8		4
		9
	7	

Daily Progress Record 15

How many did you get correct each day? Color the squares.

	Monday	Tuesday	Wednesday	Thursday	Friday
5					
4					
3					
2					
1					

1. 47 + 39 = _____

2.   834
     − 617

3. Mark the unit of measure used to measure a person's weight.

cups   pounds   meters   grams

4. Round each number to the nearest 1

49 is almost _____

21 is almost _____

5. One ice-cream cone costs 48 cents. Mark the fewest coins you would use to pay for two ice-cream cones.

1. 7 x 6 = 6 x ☐

2.   24
      15
      30
    + 25

3. 63 ☐ 36 = 99

4. Mark the cylinder.

5. If an elephant eats 200 pounds of food a day, how much will it eat in four days?

_____ pounds

Wednesday ⟨16⟩

1. 25 ÷ 5 = _____

2. $\begin{array}{r} 8 \\ \times\,7 \\ \hline \end{array}$

3. Write four number sentences using 5, 9, and 45.

_____ _____

_____ _____

4. Write an estimate for the answer to this problem.

$$89 + 67$$

_____

5. Mr. Tanaka makes birdhouses. He made 36 blue birdhouses, 24 brown, and 16 green birdhouses. How many birdhouses did he make?

_____ birdhouses

Daily Math Practice

Thursday ⟨16⟩

1. 124 – 24 = _____

2. $\begin{array}{r} 384 \\ +\,169 \\ \hline \end{array}$

3. Write these numbers in order from smallest to largest.

29   191   48   196   9

____ ____ ____ ____ ____

4. Round these numbers to the nearest 10.

27 is almost _____

62 is almost _____

5. A bag of peanuts cost Bonnie 65¢. She gave the clerk three quarters. How much change did Bonnie get back?

_____¢

Friday 〈16〉

Look at each Input and Output number.
Figure out the pattern.
Then complete the chart.

Input	Output
4	8
	18
12	24
15	
20	
	200

Daily Progress Record 〈16〉

How many did you get correct each day? Color the squares.

	Monday	Tuesday	Wednesday	Thursday	Friday
5					
4					
3					
2					
1					

1. 120 – 56 = _____

2. 270
      + 158

3. Which number is three hundred forty-six?

     a. 436   c. 346

     b. 3,460   d. 634

4. Write an odd number.

_____

5. If Vicki eats 3 pieces of fruit every day, how many days will 18 pieces of fruit last?

_____ days

1. 90 – 63 = _____

2. 3
      x 8

3. Look at the clocks. Show a half-hour later.

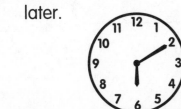 

4. 32 + 6 = 38, so ☐ – 6 = 32.

5. Arturo has 25 toy dinosaurs. His brother gave him 6 more. How many does he have now?

_____ toy dinosaurs

1. $2 \times 9 = $ _____

2. $\begin{array}{r} 153 \\ -27 \\ \hline \end{array}$

3. Expand the number.

$78 = $ ____ $+$ ____

4. Fill in the correct symbol.

$< \ = \ >$

$697 \bigcirc 796$

5. If one week has seven days, how many days are in seven weeks?

_____ days

1. $32 \div 8 = $ _____

2. $\begin{array}{r} 9 \\ \times 6 \\ \hline \end{array}$

3. Mark the cone.

4. Fill in the correct symbol.

$< \ = \ >$

$3 \times 4 \bigcirc 12 \div 3$

5. Pete had $4.50. He spent $1.42. How much money does he have left?

$_____

Friday ⟨17⟩

Amy's Schedule			
6:00	Get up	12:00	Lunch
8:00	School starts	3:00	School ends
10:30	Recess	5:00	Do homework

1. What does Amy do at 12:00? _____

2. When does Amy get up? _____

3. How long is Amy at school? _____

Daily Progress Record ⟨17⟩

How many did you get correct each day? Color the squares.

	Monday	Tuesday	Wednesday	Thursday	Friday
5					
4					
3					
2					
1					

1. $40 - 6 =$ _____

2. 574
    + 353

3. Continue the pattern.

     600   700 _____

    _____   _____

4. 6 ☐ 4 ☐ 8 = 2

5. There are 7 people in the Garcia family. Each of them ate 11 pretzels. How many pretzels did they eat?

     _____ pretzels

---

1. $9 \times 5 =$ _____

2. 286
    − 79

3. Circle the digit in the ones place. Make an **X** on the digit in the hundreds place.

     694

4. 8 cups = _____ quarts

     a. 1   b. 2   c. 3   d. 4

5. If one pencil costs Nick 9¢, how much will eight pencils cost?

     _____¢

If Nick pays with three quarters, how much change will he get back?

     _____¢

1. 4 × 8 = _____

2. 385
      + 74
      _____

3. What fraction is shaded?

  $\dfrac{\Box}{8}$

4. Write the number for two hundred fifty-three.

_____

5. Gumdrops are 2 for 8¢. How many can Angelina buy with 32¢?

_____ gumdrops

1. 32 − 6 = _____

2. 6⟌48

3. Color $\frac{1}{3}$.

☐ ☐ ☐ ☐ ☐ ☐

4. Fill in the correct symbol.

< = >

592 ◯ 586

5. Eddie had 72 jelly beans. He gave 8 jelly beans to each of his friends. How many friends got jelly beans?

_____ friends

Friday ⟨18⟩

Francie wants to give three dog bones to each of her dogs. She has five dogs. How many dog bones will Francie need? Show your answer in each box.

Use pictures to solve this problem.	Use addition to solve this problem.	Use multiplication to solve this problem.

Daily Progress Record ⟨18⟩

How many did you get correct each day? Color the squares.

	Monday	Tuesday	Wednesday	Thursday	Friday
5					
4					
3					
2					
1					

1. 75 + 22 = _____

2.   384
        – 106

3.

$\frac{1}{2}$ of 6 = _____

4. Round these numbers to the nearest hundred.

189 is almost _____

115 is almost _____

5. There were 24 dogs in the dog show. It was the first show for $\frac{1}{3}$ of the dogs. How many dogs were in their first dog show?

_____ dogs

---

1. 9 x 7 = _____

2.   86
        + 47

3. Circle the odd numbers.

23   81   18   34   65

4. 467¢ = $_____

5. Jim and Kim sell lemonade at a stand in front of their house. They charge 25 cents a cup for the lemonade. Nine people bought lemonade today. How much money did Jim and Kim collect?

$_____

1. 104 – 14 = _____

4. 4 tens and 9 ones = _____

2. 4)36

5. Write number sentences using 7, 3, and 21.

_____ X _____ = _____

_____ X _____ = _____

_____ ÷ _____ = _____

_____ ÷ _____ = _____

3. Find the perimeter of the dog's yard.

_____ feet

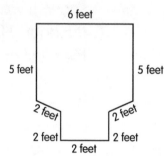

1. 36 ÷ 9 = _____

4. _____ $\frac{1}{4}$ s =

2.
```
   32
   28
 + 46
```

5. It has been snowing for three days. Monday it snowed six inches, yesterday it snowed five inches, and today it has snowed four inches. How much has it snowed?

○ less than 1 foot

○ 1 foot

○ more than 1 foot

3. Draw a different line of symmetry on each shape.

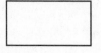

Friday ⟨19⟩

Shells Found	🐚 = 2 shells
Mark 🐚🐚🐚	Tonia 🐚🐚🐚🐚🐚
Carlos 🐚🐚🐚🐚	Mei Ling 🐚🐚

1. What is the subject of this graph? _____

2. How many shells does each symbol stand for? _____

3. How many fewer shells did Mark find than Tonia? _____

Daily Progress Record ⟨19⟩

How many did you get correct each day? Color the squares.

	Monday	Tuesday	Wednesday	Thursday	Friday
5					
4					
3					
2					
1					

1. 5 × 8 = _____

2. 819
－726

3. Color $\frac{4}{5}$.

4. 10 hundreds = _____

5. Christy has 84 stickers. She gave 35 stickers to her best friend. How many did she have left?

_____ stickers

1. 24 ÷ 3 = _____

2. 588
＋281

3. How long is the pencil?

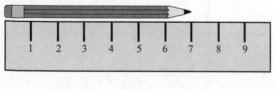

_____ cm

4. 1,450 － = 0

5. Luis can eat 1 slice of pizza in 3 minutes. How long will it take him to eat 4 slices?

_____ minutes

 EMC 6713 • © Evan-Moor Corp

Wednesday ⟨**20**⟩

1. 550 – 241 = _____

2. 5)‾50‾

3. ♡ ♡ ♡ ♡ ♡ ♡ ♡ ♡

$\frac{1}{4}$ of 8 = _____

4. What is the distance from **a** to **b** called?

○ line segment   ○ angle   ○ line

5. Sophie made 36 rag dolls to sell at the fair. She sold half of the dolls. How many dolls does she have left?

_____ rag dolls

Daily Math Practice **Thursday** ⟨**20**⟩

1. 6 × 7 = 7 × ☐

2. $3.55
     + 1.29

3. Divide this octagon into fourths.
Color $\frac{3}{4}$.

4. 684 – ☐ = 684

5. In the morning, it takes Father half an hour to dress, 15 minutes to eat breakfast, and 10 minutes to fix his lunch. If he starts at 7:00, what time will he be ready to leave for work? Show your answer on this clock.

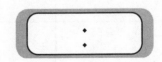

ice cream	60¢ per scoop
chocolate sauce	10¢ per slice
chocolate sauce	15¢
whipped cream	24¢
walnuts	18¢
cherry	20¢ each

2 scoops ice cream
2 banana slices
chocolate sauce
whipped cream

Make your own.

Cost $_____   Cost $_____

Daily Math Practice

Daily Progress Record 20

How many did you get correct each day? Color the squares.

	Monday	Tuesday	Wednesday	Thursday	Friday
5					
4					
3					
2					
1					

Monday ⟨21⟩

1. 18 ÷ 9 = _____

2. 845
     − 36

3. Which is the best estimate for the answer to this problem?

$$196 - 54$$

a. 100   b. 200   c. 150

4. Complete the pattern.

1,000   2,000   _____

_____   _____

5. Mel had 24¢. Then he was given a quarter from his mom and 43¢ from his dad. How much money does he have now?

_____¢

Tuesday ⟨21⟩

1. 8 × 9 = _____

2. 9,463
     + 1,025

3. Write a word problem for 3 × 4 = 12.

_____

_____

_____

4. Expand the number.

683 = ____ + ____ + ____

5. Terrie has three house cats. The Siamese weighs 4.5 kilograms, the tabby weighs 3.6 kilograms, and the Persian weighs 2.3 kilograms. How much do the cats weigh in all?

_____ kg

Wednesday ⟨21⟩

1. 1,005 + 2,025 = _____

2. 659
      − 364
      _____

3. What shape is this figure?

    a. cone

    b. sphere

    c. cylinder

4. Write an even number that is larger than 10.

_____

5. A box of popcorn costs $0.65. How much will popcorn cost for three children?

$_____

Thursday ⟨21⟩

1. 9 × 6 = _____

2. 4⟌32

3.

= $_____

4. 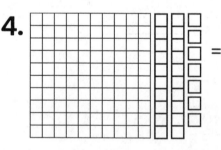 = _____

5. Whale shark eggs are about 30 cm long. Ostrich eggs are about 18 cm long. How much longer is the whale shark egg?

_____ cm

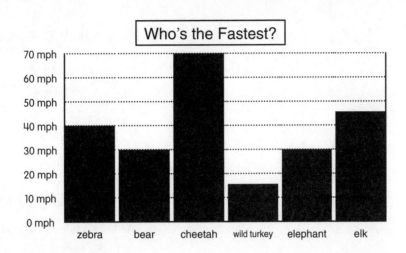

Who's the Fastest?

1. Which animal is the fastest? _____

2. Which animals run twice as fast as the wild turkey? _____

3. How much faster can the cheetah run than the elephant? _____

4. How much slower is the wild turkey than the zebra? _____

Daily Math Practice

Daily Progress Record ⟨**21**⟩

How many did you get correct each day? Color the squares.

	Monday	Tuesday	Wednesday	Thursday	Friday
5					
4					
3					
2					
1					

1. $81 \div 9 =$ _____

2. 46
     13
  + 50

3.

    a. $\frac{2}{3}$ b. $\frac{8}{6}$ c. $\frac{6}{8}$

4. $(8 + 6) + 5 =$ _____

   $8 + (6 + 5) =$ _____

5. Irma collected 24 pounds of glass. At the recycling plant, she was paid 4¢ for each pound. How much money was she paid?

_____ ¢

1. $3 \times 7 =$ _____

2. 460
   − 92

3. Fill in the correct symbol.

     <   =   >

    1,264 ◯ 1,642

4.

     = $ _____

5. It is Consuela's birthday. She got $15.75 from her grandparents, $13.00 from Aunt Mary, and $11.25 from Uncle Jose. How much money did she receive?

    $ _____

Wednesday ⟨22⟩

1. 700 − 450 = _____

2. 1,234
   + 4,827

3. Martha picked 10 baskets of peaches in an hour. How long will it take her to pick 60 baskets?

_____ hours

4. Make an **X** on the digit in the hundreds place. Draw a line under the digit in the thousands place. Circle the digit in the ones place.

6,483

5. Which unit of measure would be the best to use to measure a 10-story building?

a. inch   c. foot

b. yard   d. mile

Thursday ⟨22⟩

1. 7 × 8 = _____

2. 8)‾72‾

3. Circle the names for this fraction.

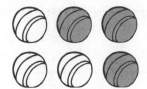

$\frac{1}{2}$ $\frac{1}{3}$ $\frac{2}{3}$ $\frac{3}{6}$

4. Circle three hundred sixty-two.

362   30,062   3,062

5. It cost $23.52 to buy lunch for the Moore family and $24.62 to buy lunch for the Miller family. How much did both families spend?

$_____

Friday ⟨22⟩

The factory makes bicycles every day. The colors of the bicycles are black, red, blue, green, and purple. Red bikes are the favorite of most children. How many days would it take the factory to make 500 bicycles?

Which sentence is needed in order to answer the question?

a. More boys than girls ride bikes.

b. The factory is open 10 hours a day.

c. The factory can make 100 bikes every day.

Now answer the question.

_____ days

Daily Progress Record ⟨22⟩

How many did you get correct each day? Color the squares.

	Monday	Tuesday	Wednesday	Thursday	Friday
5					
4					
3					
2					
1					

EMC 6713 • © Evan-Moor Cor

1. $63 \div 7 =$ _____

2.   536
     $- 274$

3.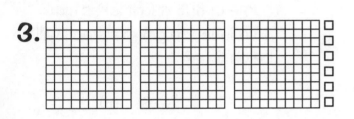

     $=$ _____

4. Circle the even numbers.

     16   21   44   38   57

5. A boa is three meters long.
A python is 197 centimeters long.

Which snake is longer?

_____

How much longer?

_____

---

1. $10 \times 6 =$ _____

2.   555
     $+ 168$

3. There are 20 soldiers in a row. In what place is soldier number 12?

   ○ second   ○ twentieth   ○ twelfth

4. Where does the decimal belong?

     $1260

a. $1.260   b. $126.0   c. $12.60

5. Liza made 240 popcorn balls. She put eight popcorn balls into each box. How many boxes did she use?

_____ boxes

1. 7 x 7 = _____

2.   245
        520
      + 315

3. Spend: $2.75   Pay with: $5.00

Change: $_____

4. Write the missing numbers.

1,250 1,300 1,350 _____

_____ _____

5. School starts at 8:55. If Wade leaves home at 8:15 and it takes him 35 minutes to get to school, will he be on time?

yes   no

---

1. 65 – 15 – 20 = _____

2. 6⟌42

3. Fill in the correct symbol.

< = >

35 + 15 ◯ 75 – 40

4. What time will it be in 20 minutes?

5. Greg has a savings account at the bank. Every week he puts half of his allowance in the bank. He gets $4.0 allowance. How much will he save i ten weeks?

$ _____

    EMC 6713 • © Evan-Moor Cor

Friday ⟨23⟩

Hot dogs come in packages of 10.

Number of Packages	1	2	3	4	5	6	7	8
Number of Hot Dogs	10	20						

Daily Math Practice

Daily Progress Record ⟨23⟩

How many did you get correct each day? Color the squares.

	Monday	Tuesday	Wednesday	Thursday	Friday
5					
4					
3					
2					
1					

1. $4 \times 2 \times 6 =$ _____

2.   328
   − 69

3. Which shape has 8 sides of equal length?

   pentagon   hexagon

   octagon   rhombus

4. Continue the pattern.

   14   21   28 ____ ____ ____

   ____ ____

5. I am an even number between 0 and 9. I am less than 6 and more than 3. What number am I?

   _____

1. $30 \div 6 =$ _____

2.   300
     200
   + 500

3. Is this picture symmetrical?

   yes

   no

4. Round these numbers to the nearest hundred.

   193 is almost _____

   230 is almost _____

5. The diameter of the planet Venus is about 650 km smaller than the diameter of Earth. If Earth's diameter is about 13,000 km, what is the diameter of Venus?

   _____ km

                                          EMC 6713 • © Evan-Moor Corp

Wednesday ⟨24⟩

1. 54 ÷ 9 = _____

2. $4.65
  − 3.79
     _____

3. Show a quarter to 12 on the clock.

4. 927 = _____ hundreds _____ tens

_____ ones

5. Evan can do a sit-up every 5 seconds. How long will it take him to do 24 sit-ups?

_____ minutes

Thursday ⟨24⟩

1. 12 x 2 = _____

2. 2,086
  + 1,529
     _____

3. Draw two shapes that are congruent.

4. Fill in the correct symbol.

< = >

16 ounces ◯ 1 pound

5. Rama and her friends each ate 7 cherries. A total of 28 cherries were eaten. How many children ate the cherries?

_____ children

Friday ⟨24⟩

Complete the table.
How many treats will each person get?

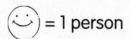 = 1 person

There are 25 pretzels.	☺ ☺ ☺ ☺ ☺	_____ pretzels each
There are 24 jelly beans.	☺ ☺ ☺ ☺	_____ jelly beans each
There are 18 cookies.	☺ ☺ ☺	_____ cookies each
There are 16 peanuts.	☺ ☺	_____ peanuts each

Daily Math Practice

Daily Progress Record ⟨24⟩

How many did you get correct each day? Color the squares.

	Monday	Tuesday	Wednesday	Thursday	Friday
5					
4					
3					
2					
1					

1. 256 + 437 = _____

2. 30
    x 3

3. Color $\frac{1}{4}$ of the shape.

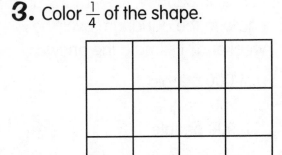

4. Continue the pattern.

3 5 8 10 ____ ____ ____

5. Cary, Terry, and Mary each have 6 pieces of gum. How much gum do they have in all? Mark the **two** ways you can find the answer.

○ add   ○ subtract

○ divide   ○ multiply

---

1. $5.54 – $2.75 = _____

2. 2⟌40

3. Tomas bought 7 packages of gum. There were 9 sticks of gum in each package. How many sticks of gum did Tomas buy?

_____ sticks of gum

4. 46 + ☐ = 60

5. What is the perimeter of this building?

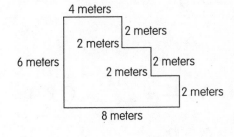

_____ meters

Wednesday ⟨25⟩

1. 364 – 192 = _____

2.   1,462
        3,017
    + 5,236
    _____

3. Draw three different shapes with four corners and four sides.

4. (2 x 2) x 3 = _____

    2 x (2 x 3) = _____

5. Five hundred and ninety people came to the aquarium on Saturday. Three hundred and eighty people came on Sunday. How many people came to the aquarium over the weekend? Estimate the answer.

   a. 1,000 people
   b.   500 people
   c.   900 people

Thursday ⟨25⟩

1. 28 ÷ 7 = _____

2.   14
   x 2
   ____

3. 0 x 4 = ____   0 x 9 = ____

   0 x 2 = ____

   Any number multiplied by 0 = ____.

4. Fill in the correct symbol.

     <   =   >

    9,050 ◯ 5,090

5. Write a word problem for 15 – 10 = 5

_____

_____

_____

Friday ⟨25⟩

Baskets of strawberries come in three sizes. Small baskets hold 15 strawberries. A middle-size basket holds 30 strawberries. The largest baskets hold 45 strawberries. Jacob bought three baskets.

What is the smallest number of strawberries he might have?

_____ strawberries

What is the largest number of strawberries Jacob might have?

_____ strawberries

Daily Math Practice

Daily Progress Record ⟨25⟩

How many did you get correct each day? Color the squares.

	Monday	Tuesday	Wednesday	Thursday	Friday
5					
4					
3					
2					
1					

Monday ⟨26⟩

1. $6.50 + $6.50 = _____

2.   325
     – 68

3. 1 x 5 = _____   1 x 9 = _____

Any number times 1

= _____.

4. Fill in the correct symbol.

< = >

$9 \times 3 \bigcirc 9 \div 3$

5. Frank raises rabbits to sell. He has 8 does. Each doe has 6 babies. How many rabbits does he have?

_____ rabbits

Tuesday ⟨26⟩

1. 11 x 7 = _____

2.   9,087
     – 3,647

3. Write three names for 20.

____ + ____   ____ x ____

____ – ____

4. Give an estimation for the answer to 212 + 486.

_____

5. Kira has 9 bags of shells. Each bag holds 9 shells. How many shells does Kira have?

_____ shells

EMC 6713 • © Evan-Moor Corp.

Wednesday ⟨26⟩

1. $48 \div 6 =$ _____

2. $$\begin{array}{r} \$4.75 \\ -\ \ 2.25 \\ \hline \end{array}$$

3. six hundred ninety-seven

     a. 60,097   c. 697

     b. 6,097   d. none of these

4. Fill in the correct symbol.

         <   =   >

     \$5 ◯ 8 quarters

5. How many pieces of gum can Dina buy if each one costs 4 cents and she has a quarter, a dime, and a penny?

     _____ pieces of gum

Thursday ⟨26⟩

1. $5,066 + 1,749 =$ _____

2. $7\overline{)35}$

3. Fill in the missing numbers.

     1,000   1,100   1,200 _____

     _____   _____   _____

4. $54 \;\boxed{}\; 9 = 6$

5. There were 48 children at the picnic. Teams of equal size were formed to play games. How many children were on each of the 6 teams?

     _____ children

Aunt Emma planted 6 rows of 9 flowers and 8 rows of 7 flowers in her garden this year. Last year she planted 100 flowers. Did she plant more or less flowers this year?

     more   less

How many more or less?

_____ flowers

Daily Progress Record 〈26〉

How many did you get correct each day? Color the squares.

	Monday	Tuesday	Wednesday	Thursday	Friday
5					
4					
3					
2					
1					

1. 10 x 7 = _____

2. 836
+ 475

3.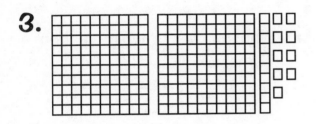

= _____

4. Continue the pattern.

150 175 200 ____ ____ ____

5. Tanisha is going to buy one cookie for each student in her class. There are 8 cookies in each package. How many packages will she need to buy for 24 students?

_____ packages

1. 36 ÷ 6 = _____

2. 224
163
+ 32

3. 1 thousand + 6 hundreds + 3 tens

+ 4 ones = _____

4. Where does the decimal belong in ten dollars and six cents?

$1006

5. A fisherman caught 24 fish. He gave the same number of fish to 6 of his friends. How many fish did each friend get?

_____ fish

1. 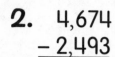 7⟌49

2.   4,674
     − 2,493

3. Circle the numbers that equal 1.

$\frac{2}{2}$ $\frac{5}{6}$ $\frac{8}{8}$ $\frac{4}{4}$ $\frac{3}{6}$

4. What time is it?

_____ minutes after _____

_____ minutes before _____

5. What number is two more than 7 times 6?

_____

---

1. 21 x 3 = _____

2.   455
     − 170

3. Mrs. Chan hired four boys to paint her fence. She paid each boy 12 dollars. How much did it cost her to have the fence painted?

$_____

4. Expand the number.

471 = _____ + _____ + _____

5. What is the area of this rectangle?

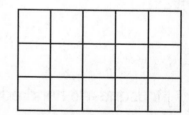

_____ square units

   EMC 6713 • © Evan-Moor Corp.

Friday 27

Number these in order from the least amount to the greatest amount.

5   12   19 ⬤   3 ⬤   12 ⬤

___   ___   ___   ___   ___

Daily Progress Record <27>

How many did you get correct each day? Color the squares.

	Monday	Tuesday	Wednesday	Thursday	Friday
5					
4					
3					
2					
1					

1. 10 × 8 = _____

2. 6,307
    + 984

3. 7 thousands, 8 hundreds, and
    5 ones =

    _____

4. Had:

Spent: $1.75

Had left: $_____

5. One cup of popcorn kernels make
    four cups of popped corn. There
    are eight cups of kernels in the
    bag. How many cups of popped
    corn will Doug make?

    _____ cups

1. 72 ÷ 9 = _____

2. 964
    − 632

3. Color $\frac{2}{5}$.

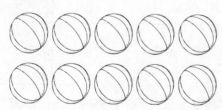

4. $\frac{7}{10}$ =

   a. 0.7   b. 0.5   c. 1.07

5. Craig's team had batting practice
    today. Each player got to swing at
    the ball 7 times. If 9 players came
    to practice, how many balls were
    pitched?

    _____ balls

1. 5,265 – 1,638 = _____

2. 8)64

3. Write the time 5 minutes later.

4:20 _____   6:15 _____

9:25 _____   2:40 _____

4. Circle the largest number.

10,560   10,422   10,920

5. The ball game started at 10:00. It ended at 1:30. How long did the ball game last?

a. 1 hour

b. 3 and a half hours

c. 1 and a half hours

---

1. twenty + thirty + ten = _____

2.   32
   x 4

3. Joan can bake 1 dozen cookies in 15 minutes. How long will it take her to bake 3 dozen cookies?

_____ minutes

4. 45 ÷ 9 = 5, so 45 ÷ 5 = ☐ .

5. Are these shapes congruent?

    yes   no

Explain your answer.

_____

_____

_____

Friday ⟨28⟩

Tara collected information about when the students in her class were born.
Record the information on this line graph.

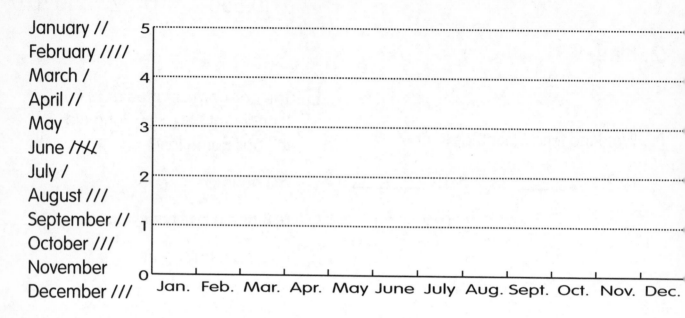

January //
February ////
March /
April //
May
June /////
July /
August ///
September //
October ///
November
December ///

Daily Progress Record ⟨28⟩

How many did you get correct each day? Color the squares.

	Monday	Tuesday	Wednesday	Thursday	Friday
5					
4					
3					
2					
1					

EMC 6713 • © Evan-Moor Corp.

1. 6,805 + 2,300 = _____

2. 32
     x 3

3. Circle the digit in the thousands place. Underline the digit in the tens place.

12,463

4. There are _____ centimeters in a meter.

5. Complete the number sentences. Use only 3, 4, and 5.

____ + ____ x ____ = 27

____ x ____ − ____ = 11

____ x ____ + ____ = 17

____ x ____ x ____ = 60

1. 40 ÷ 5 = _____

2. 403
     − 268

3. Write the number for twelve dollars and sixty-eight cents.

$_____

4. (6 x 2) x 1 = _____

6 x (2 x 1) = _____

5. It costs $8.25 to buy a ticket to the basketball game. How much would three tickets cost?

$_____

Wednesday ⟨29⟩

1. $7\overline{)56}$

2. fifty – twenty = _____

3. Order these fractions from smallest to largest.

$$\frac{1}{2} \qquad \frac{1}{6} \qquad \frac{1}{3} \qquad \frac{1}{4}$$

____ – ____ ____ ____

4. $81 \ \boxed{} \ 9 = 9$

5. How many pears are there in $2\frac{1}{2}$ dozen?

_____ pears

Thursday ⟨29⟩

1. $20 \times 4 =$ _____

2. $\begin{array}{r} \frac{11}{12} \\ -\frac{10}{12} \end{array}$

3. Count by ones to fill in the missing numbers.

7,804 _____   3,069 _____

5,590 _____   1,999 _____

4. $\frac{1}{4}$ of 12 = _____

5. Erika's class went to the zoo. They saw 54 different animals. Half of the animals came from Africa. How many animals were from Africa?

_____ animals

  EMC 6713 • © Evan-Moor Corp.

Friday 〈29〉

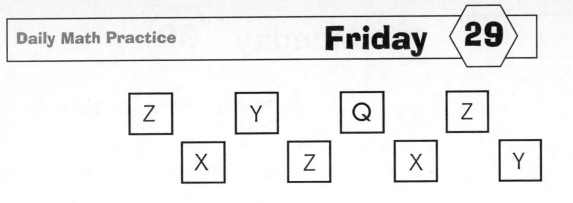

Which letter is **most likely** to be picked without looking?

_____

Which letter is **least likely** to be picked without looking?

_____

Daily Math Practice

Daily Progress Record 〈29〉

How many did you get correct each day? Color the squares.

	Monday	Tuesday	Wednesday	Thursday	Friday
5					
4					
3					
2					
1					

1. $\frac{4}{6}$
$+\frac{1}{6}$

2. $9\overline{)63}$

3. $\frac{6}{10} =$

    ◯ 6.0   ◯ 0.6   ◯ 10.6

4. Which number is nine thousand forty?

  a. 940   c. 9,004

  b. 9,040   d. none of these

5. Father is building a square fence around the garden. Each side is 8 meters long. What is the perimeter of the fence?

_____ meters

---

1. 13 × 4 = _____

2.   334
  − 95

3. 27 ÷ 9 = 3, so 9 × 3 = ☐

4. What fraction is shaded?

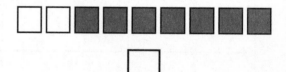

5. A gray whale dove 129 feet on its first dive, 360 feet on its second dive, and 277 feet on its third dive. How many feet did the whale dive in all?

_____ feet

EMC 6713 · © Evan-Moor Corp

Wednesday ⬡30

1. 24 ÷ 8 = _____

2.   609
       − 345

3. How many thousands in 24,692?

_____ thousands

4. Count by nines.

___ ___ ___ ___ ___

___ ___ ___ ___ ___

5. A farmer brought 15 watermelons to the picnic. Each watermelon was cut into 6 slices. If each person got one slice, how many people ate watermelon?

_____ people

Thursday ⬡30

1. 7 × 9 = _____

2.   373
       + 479

3. Draw a symmetrical shape.

4. Complete the pattern.

1   5   2   6   ___   ___   ___

5. Bill and Kathy are building a doghouse for Buddy. They went to the lumberyard and spent $22.42. If they gave the clerk $24.00, how much change did they receive?

$_____

1. Circle the right angle.

2. Circle the angle that is greater than a right angle.

3. Circle the angle that is less than a right angle.

Daily Math Practice

Daily Progress Record ⟨30⟩

How many did you get correct each day? Color the squares.

	Monday	Tuesday	Wednesday	Thursday	Friday
5					
4					
3					
2					
1					

Monday ⟨31⟩

1. 81 − 66 = _____

2. 465
      + 877
      ‾‾‾‾‾

3. Write two fractions for this picture.

4. Expand this number.

2,086

_____

5. A sea otter ate 35 sea stars in the last 5 days. She ate the same number of sea stars each day. How many sea stars did she eat each day?

_____ sea stars

Tuesday ⟨31⟩

1. 42 × 2 = _____

2. $2\frac{1}{3}$
      $+2\frac{1}{3}$
      ‾‾‾‾‾

3. Round these numbers to the nearest ten.

93 is almost _____

38 is almost _____

4. Number these lengths in order from shortest to longest.

2 ft.   1 yd.   9 ft.   18 in.   2 yd.

___ ___ ___ ___ ___

5. If there are 365 days in one year, how many days are there in three years?

_____ days

Wednesday ⟨31⟩

1. 24 + 12 + 16 = _____

2.   28
       x 3

3. Draw a line segment. Label it **ab**.

4. Write the number for sixteen dollars and eighty-four cents.

$_____

5. Allan earned $10.00 for mowing lawns. He bought a birthday present for his sister that cost $5.50. How much money did he have left?

$_____

Thursday ⟨31⟩

1. 5)26

2.   2,568
       + 1,425

3. How many inches are there in 5 feet?

_____ inches

4. Which number is ninety-four thousand five hundred?

a. 90,450   c. 9,450

b. 95,400   d. 94,500

5. A kite costs $9.60. Today it is on sale at $\frac{1}{3}$ off. What is the sale price of the kite?

$_____

   EMC 6713 • © Evan-Moor Corp.

Friday ⟨31⟩

Fill in the missing numbers on the chart.

whole number	fraction	decimal
4 cents	$\frac{4}{100}$	$0.04
12 cents		
25 cents		

Daily Progress Record ⟨31⟩

How many did you get correct each day? Color the squares.

	Monday	Tuesday	Wednesday	Thursday	Friday
5					
4					
3					
2					
1					

1. 370 – 190 = _____

2.
$$3\frac{6}{12}$$
$$+7\frac{4}{12}$$

3. Color boxes to show the fraction $\frac{8}{12}$.

4. How many quarts are in $4\frac{1}{2}$ gallons

_____ quarts

5. Shannon's birthday is on May 10th. Paul's birthday is two weeks later. What is the date of Paul's birthday?

_____

---

1. 29 ÷ 7 = _____

2.
$$662$$
$$-275$$

3. Circle the shapes that are congruent.

4. Write the number word for 163.

_____

5. Bernard sells fishing worms. A box of 50 worms costs $2.95. Mr. Reyes bought 8 boxes. How many worms did he get?

_____ worms

EMC 6713 • © Evan-Moor Corp

Wednesday 〈32〉

1. 6⟌55

2. 426
  x 3

3. Which shape is symmetrical?

4. Write the number for three thousand nine hundred thirty-four.

_____

5. Dr. Light performed an operation that started at 2:30. It lasted 2 hours and 20 minutes. At what time was the operation over?

○ 4:30   ○ 4:45   ○ 4:50

Thursday 〈32〉

1. 74 ÷ 9 = _____

2. 2,317
      + 1,925

3. Fill in the correct symbol.

< = >

16,439 ◯ 18,006

4. Write the number 352 in expanded form.

_____

5. Can Ralph buy a mitt that costs $17.50 if he has this amount of money?

yes   no

Every afternoon the children in nursery school have a snack. Today 6 children had a fruit snack. Each plate contained 3 apple slices, 6 banana bits, 2 orange pieces, and 5 grapes. How many pieces of fruit did the cook have to prepare in all?

_____ pieces of fruit

How many did you get correct each day? Color the squares.

	Monday	Tuesday	Wednesday	Thursday	Friday
5					
4					
3					
2					
1					

1. 649 + 138 = _____

2. 67
    x 5
    ___

3. Draw an octagon.

4.

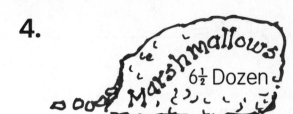

6½ Dozen

= _____ marshmallows

5. The game lasted 3 hours and 16 minutes. It began at 1:30. At what time did the game end?

○ 4:06   ○ 4:16   ○ 4:46

---

1. 28 ÷ 5 = _____

2. 643
   − 475
   ____

3. Circle 0.5 of the stars.

4. 200 + 90 + 8 = _____

5. A knot is a measure of speed used by ships. It is 6,076.1 feet per hour. If a whale is swimming at 2 knots, how many feet will it travel after 1 hour?

_____ feet

Wednesday ⬡33

1. 34 x 3 = _____

2.   4,736
     − 3,510
   _____

3. Find the area.

[grid rectangle]

_____ square units

4. (5 x 2) x 6 = _____

5 x (2 x 6) = _____

5. On Sunday 13 boats were in a race. There were 8 boats with 3 sailors each, 4 boats with 2 sailors each, and one boat with 5 sailors. How many sailors were in the race?

_____ sailors

Thursday ⬡33

1. 7)‾44‾

2.   8,336
     + 1,937
   _____

3. Fill in the correct symbol.

< = >

$\frac{1}{2}$ ◯ $\frac{3}{6}$

4. Circle the spinner that is equally likely to land on black or white.

5. Add together the numbers on the fourth, second, and sixth apples. Divide that amount by three. What is the quotient?

_____

Friday 〈**33**〉

Mr. White asked his 24 students, "How do you get to school?"
He collected these answers:

   walk–12   ride bike–3

   ride bus–6   ride in a car–3

Color in the circle graph to record the information.

   walk–red   bike–blue

   bus–yellow   car–green

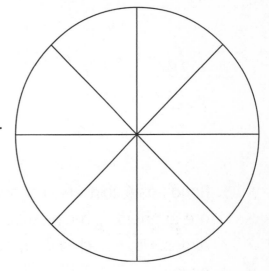

Daily Math Practice

Daily Progress Record 〈**33**〉

How many did you get correct each day? Color the squares.

	Monday	Tuesday	Wednesday	Thursday	Friday
5					
4					
3					
2					
1					

Monday ⟨34⟩

1. 24 x 5 = _____

2.   386
   + 292

3. Rona has 6 coins. Half of her coins are quarters, $\frac{1}{3}$ are nickels, and $\frac{1}{6}$ are dimes. How much money does she have?

_____ ¢

4. Write four number sentences using 3, 7, and 21.

_____

_____

_____

_____

5. Write the number word for 729.

_____

Tuesday ⟨34⟩

1. 65 ÷ 5 = _____

2.   3,980
   + 2,356

3. 2 thousands, 5 hundreds, 6 ones =

_____

4. It is 6:00 P.M. What time will it be in 8 hours?

○ 8:00 A.M.
○ 2:00 P.M.
○ 2:00 A.M.

5. Model cars that cost $2.95 are on sale for $1.80. How much could Dennis save if he buys two cars on sale?

$_____

Wednesday ⟨34⟩

1. $9\overline{)59}$

2. 826
− 469

3. _____ corners

_____ edges

_____ faces

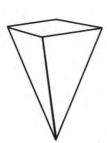

4. (9 x 7) x 2 = _____

9 x (7 x 2) = _____

5. It is 3 hours earlier in Oregon than in Maine. If it is 2:30 P.M. in Maine, what time is it in Oregon?

_____

Thursday ⟨34⟩

1. $8\overline{)49}$

2. 4,146
+ 3,289

3. Make an **X** on the digit in the tens place. Circle the digit in the thousands place.

9,782

4. Circle the polygon that does <u>not</u> have a right angle.

5. An explorer discovered a treasure chest. It contained 150 bags of silver coins. He got to keep one-third of the bags of coins. How many bags did he get to keep?

_____ bags

Friday 〈34〉

Two of the numbers below have a sum of 10 and a product of 24.

2 3 4 5 6

What is their difference?

Show your work here.

Write your answer here.

Daily Progress Record 〈34〉

How many did you get correct each day? Color the squares.

	Monday	Tuesday	Wednesday	Thursday	Friday
5					
4					
3					
2					
1					

EMC 6713 • © Evan-Moor Corp

1. 3)‾72‾

2.   3,148
   + 4,907

3. How much of this group is shaded?

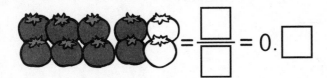

4. How are a cube and a square alike?

_____

different?

_____

5. Trina has a paper route. She delivers papers to 35 homes every day. How many papers does she deliver in a week?

_____ papers

1. $45 \times 5 =$ _____

2. $4\frac{6}{10}$
   $-1\frac{3}{10}$

3. Circle the names for 54.

   6×9 $96 - 32$ fifty-four

   $100 \div 2$ 9×6 $16 + 38$

4. Which **two** units of measure would be the best to measure the weight of an elephant?

   ○ kilograms   ○ grams
   ○ ounces   ○ pounds

5. How many hours in a day?   _____

hours in a week?   _____

Wednesday 35

1. 43 x 8 = _____

2.   576
      − 289

3. Complete this pattern.

   3   6   12   24   ____   ____   ____

4. Fill in the correct symbol.

   <   =   >

   18 inches ◯ 2 feet

5. Kris sent party invitations to a dozen friends. The invitations cost $1.95 for six. How much did he spend on invitations?

   $_____

Thursday 35

1. 30 ÷ 8 = _____

2.   426
      + 393

3. Write the number 1,962 in expanded form.

   _____

4. 96 ÷ 8 = 12, so 12 x 8 = ☐ .

5. Sammy is collecting newspapers to raise money for the Boys and Girls Club. Last week he collected 10 pounds of newspapers every day for 4 days. He was paid 12¢ a pound for the papers. How much did he get paid in all?

   $_____

          EMC 6713 • © Evan-Moor Corp

Use the information on the map to work each problem.

A salesman travels from Springfield to Willow Grove every day. Then he drives on to Myrtle Lake, Eagle Mountain Park, and back to Springfield. How far does he drive every day?

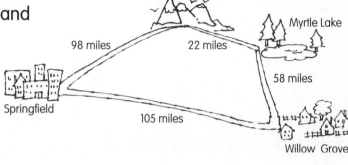

_____ miles

The salesman has only enough gas to drive 90 miles. Can he drive from Willow Grove to Eagle Mountain Park without stopping to refuel?

yes   no

Daily Math Practice

Daily Progress Record ⬡35⬡

How many did you get correct each day? Color the squares.

	Monday	Tuesday	Wednesday	Thursday	Friday
5					▓
4					▓
3					▓
2					
1					

1. 106 – 17 = _____

2. 128
 x 7

3. Mark the rectangular prism.

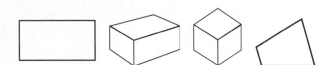

4. Fill in the correct symbol.

< = >

9,462 ◯ 6,936

5. There were 826 people on a train. At the first stop, 93 got off and 76 got on. How many people are on the train now?

_____ people

---

1. 4)56‾

2. 980
  362
 + 659

3. Circle the digit in the hundreds place. Make an **X** on the digit in the ones place.

14,608

4. How many ounces are in a pound?

_____ ounces

5. How many of each of these coins would it take to make $2.00?

_____ half dollars = $2.00

_____ quarters = $2.00

_____ dimes = $2.00

_____ nickels = $2.00

EMC 6713 • © Evan-Moor Corp.

1. 29 × 3 = _____

2.   9,063
       − 4,135

3. $\frac{1}{4}$ of 16 = _____

4. What time is it?

_____ minutes before _____

5. What number equals the centimeters in a meter minus the inches in a yard?

_____

1. 90 ÷ 6 = _____

2. Round to the nearest 1,000.

2,805 _____

3. Write the number for fifty thousand.

_____

4. 32 ÷ 8 = 4, so 8 × ☐ = 32.

5. The farmer's prize pig had six piglets. One weighed 8 pounds, four weighed 6 pounds each, and one weighed 5 pounds. What is the total weight of the piglets?

_____ pounds

Connect the line segments to make a geometric shape.

$\overline{BG}$ $\overline{BC}$ $\overline{FA}$

$\overline{CD}$ $\overline{DG}$ $\overline{FG}$

$\overline{EF}$ $\overline{DE}$ $\overline{AB}$

What shape did you make?

_____

A B

F G •C

E D

Daily Math Practice

Daily Progress Record ⟨36⟩

How many did you get correct each day? Color the squares.

	Monday	Tuesday	Wednesday	Thursday	Friday
5					
4					
3					
2					
1					

EMC 6713 • © Evan-Moor Corp.

How to Solve
Word Problems

 Read the problem carefully. Think about what it says.

 Look for clue words. The clue words will tell you which operation to use—addition, subtraction, multiplication, or division. Hint: Sometimes you will use more than one operation.

 Solve the problem.

 Check your work. Make sure your answer makes sense.

Clue Words

Add	Subtract	Multiply	Divide
in all	how much more	times	parts
altogether	more than	product of	equal parts
total	less than	multiplied by	separated
sum	are left	by (with measurements or dimensions)	divided by
both	take away		quotient of
plus	difference	area	a fraction of
	fewer		average